WORKSHOP-IN-YOUR-POCKET

Write Business

JP ROBINSON

About the Author

JP Robinson began writing as a teen and gained experience in the marketing field doing promotional work for multi-million dollar medical facilities and non-profit groups. He is an international speaker, educator, and prolific author of both fiction and non-fiction.

JP also conducts writing seminars in various parts of the country and heads Logos Publications, LLC, an emerging publishing and book marketing team.

When he isn't writing or teaching, JP loves spending time with his wonderful wife and kids.

Workshop-In-Your-Pocket

Write

History

A Historical Author's Guide to Crafting Blazing Stories

JP Robinson

What people are saying:

WORKSHOP-IN-YOUR-POCKET

Write Business

JP ROBINSON

Table of Contents

Introduction

In 2019 I stood in front of a captive audience of writers, trying to convey a fundamental point that many traditional and self-published authors have realized is true. For weeks I had wrestled with my computer, determined to give my future listeners the information they needed to make the next step in their writing career a step in the right direction Now the time had come and I was ready to shake their literary worlds with four words.

It's a simple truth, but one that continues to escape many who aim to put their words in print. It's a reality that has sent the publishing industry reeling, made the fortunes of some and, no doubt, bankrupted others. Simply put, the truth is this: **the game has changed**.

The dramatic uptick in the self-publishing industry means lower barriers to entry. Thanks to platforms such as Kindle Direct Publishing (KDP), Lulu, Kobo and others, literally anyone with an internet connection can become a published author. But this seemingly incredible opportunity comes at a price. No, I don't mean one of dollars and cents—although many authors do spend an incredible amount of money to get a product listed on Amazon—I mean the cost of discovery.

With literally millions of titles available online, quality authors face an uphill battle finding and keeping the readers their books deserve. In the modern era, it is not enough to be a talented writer; you must also be a good entrepreneur. So how can you, as an author, see a return on your investment (be it time, money or both)?

That's where this book comes in.

Write Business is the second in a series of short, effective author self-help titles called **Workshop-In-Your-Pocket**. It is a simple, easy-to-read guide that provides solid strategies to help you:

- Understand current trends in the publishing world

- Develop an author-friendly business mentality

- Learn essential marketing terms and techniques specially formatted for writers

- Grow your author platform and build a writing system that pays on it

I don't promise that you'll be on the NYT best-seller list or that you will become a millionaire overnight. This book is for practical people who are willing to learn, work, and hone their craft both as a writer and as an entrepreneur. I'm going to avoid getting too "techie" but there are key marketing phrases that you'll encounter throughout this book. I've included a short glossary at the end for quick reference.

I conduct writing seminars in various parts of the country and have realized that there's simply never enough time to do justice to each topic. So, I've put it together in a book that you can reference time and again. It's formatted to give you the workshop experience but includes more detailed information that you can peruse at your own pace.

At the end of each chapter, I've included a short synopsis of the main points as well as questions tailored to take your manuscript to the next level.

Write well. Write business.

JP Robinson

CHAPTER 1:

The Write Mentality

Frank is a fitness coach who's written a book on static stretching versus dynamic stretching. Believe it or not, there's an audience for that. Knowing when to stretch and how to do it is apparently critical to an effective workout. And Frank has the know-how and experience necessary to revolutionize the fitness industry.

He's uploaded his book, *Stretch Power,* to KDP and is waiting for his first sale.

Ten minutes later he hits refresh.

Hmm... still no sales.

Frank gets up, does some stretches, goes for a run and one hour later checks again.

Nada.

Something must be wrong with the system.

But Frank is into fitness so he knows that perseverance is key. Tomorrow, things will change, he's sure of it.

But one day becomes a week. A week turns into a month. A month degenerates into a year without a single sale on Amazon's mammoth platform.

And Frank is crushed.

What's the problem?

While his content might be awesome and there are probably readers out there who'll jump on what he's got to say, Frank's approach to his writing is a hobby mentality and not a business mentality. And hobbies tend to produce sporadic income, if any at all.

Like Frank, many authors like the thought of making money from writing but don't understand how to make it happen.

Everything begins long before you hit "upload" on KDP, hand your manuscript over to a literary agent, or give it to a hybrid publishing company. It actually begins from time you start thinking about writing a book.

A hobbyist's writing mentality is something like this.

I'm writing a book but I don't know when I'll finish it. I don't have any set writing hours but, I think I can crank out maybe an hour a week. My book's for everybody, I mean it's totally, like, the best book ever!

I'm not one to judge in this regard but the approach you want to apply to your writing is more like this.

I'm writing a book for young adults, ages 13-18. Boys will be really drawn to the male protagonist but girls will also enjoy it because of the accompanying female lead. I've committed to writing at least an hour per weekday and, on the weekends, I'll put in an additional 3-4 hours. I'm laying out a basic marketing plan, including finding a critique group, and will continue to develop it as my book takes shape.

In both scenarios, the authors may have an awesome work up their writing sleeves. Their wordsmithing qualities may be superb. But the second author stands a much better chance at achieving a return on his investment because his mentality is more in line with that of an entrepreneur than an author.

Let me clarify here.

It's not enough for you to be a good author—not anymore. The "write" mentality is that of an entrepreneur, or as I like to call it, a **writerpreneur.** This is especially true if you are indie publishing your titles, however, it is a fact that traditionally published authors are also finding it necessary to incorporate strategic marketing techniques ... techniques that I'll share in the following pages.

Takeaway:

1. The game has changed. To be successful, authors need to incorporate effective, money-saving strategies to maximize their ROI (return on investment).

2. Success begins with the "write" mentality. Think of your writing as a business not a hobby with regulated writing hours, organization. Be proactive in your approach to see results to avoid getting lost in the online publishing labyrinth.

Personal Reflection:

1. How seriously do you take your writing on a scale of 1-5 (with 1 being a hobby and 5 being a business mentality)? Why is that?

2. What steps will you take to change or reinforce your business mentality?

CHAPTER 2:

Writing That Sells

Best-sellers are no accident. Neither are they random coincidences. They are nothing but the deliberate products of human ingenuity, research and planning.

I once interviewed a literary agent from one of America's best agencies. I was curious to know what are the most important characteristics of a genre-specific best-seller. While there is no set formula to end up on the New York Times best-seller list, the agent indicated that what's going on in society, and its role in a book's content can play a big part in how successful a book becomes.[1]

Some authors approach the business from the standpoint that they *must* get their message or their story out to the public no matter what. While that may be true, the results you obtain may be disappointing, so much so that you give up on writing altogether.

The biblical proverb "to everything there is a season" also holds true in writing successful books. Why reinvent the wheel? You want to write about what's

1 Read the interview on my site: **JPRobinsonbooks.com**

trending, creatively encapsulating current themes into your work. This applies whether you're writing fiction or non-fiction because, in truth, all good writing is based on fact.

For example, a hot topic at the time of this book's publication is the controversy over the expansion or limitation of the abortion laws on the state-level. Regardless of whether your stance on the issue is conservative, liberal or something in-between, you have an opinion and people may pay to hear (or should I say, *read*) it.

Yes, no matter where you stand there will be those who don't appreciate what you have to say, but that isn't the point. The point is that people are typing keywords into Google, Amazon, Facebook and Twitter that relate to your topic. Some are searching to find opinions that justify their ideologies. Others may be searching to find opinions with which they disagree. In both cases, there is a potential market.

Writing that sells capitalizes on themes that interest readers one way or another. It's for you as an author to creatively weave those themes into your work-in-progress then market them effectively so the world can hear what you have to say.

Writer Recap: You want to write about what's trending, creatively encapsulating current themes into your work.

As time goes along and you build up an audience of loyal fans, perhaps then would be a time to write that Western romance or that memoir. But at first, you want to write about what's on everyone's mind. Now this doesn't necessarily have to be the latest trending hashtag on Twitter. There are immortal themes that can easily be applied to virtually any manuscript.

The search for meaning, (mis)adventures when coming-of-age, dealing with grief and crises of faith, for example, can all form the basis for writing that sells because virtually every human on the planet has experienced these issues at some point in his or her life.

I'm going to take this moment to segway into another aspect of this important topic. Question: have you ever noticed that whenever a popular movie comes out, there are about a dozen others that release on a similar theme? I mean, how many different versions of *Beauty and the Beast* can there be? But film producers (or their marketing teams) know that if there *was* a market for that movie, those same moviegoers will likely watch *their* adaptation of the same topic.

The same can be said for amazing books. If a certain character profile or theme is proving popular, you may want consider adding a similar title to your own writing portfolio. I want to add a word of caution here and it's very important that you don't miss this.

Be sure you are writing about a topic or in a genre that genuinely interests you and that you have thoroughly researched.

Readers have this bizarre and slightly threatening ability to tell when an author is bored with what he or she is writing. It somehow leaks into our word choices and, like a blood clot, stymies the flow of our inspiration. Furthermore, if you simply jump on the bandwagon of a popular genre without doing appropriate research and preparation, the reviews you receive will probably not be favorable and will not endear you to readers at large.

So consider popular genres or trending topics as a possibility to explore but, by no means am I encouraging you to write about a topic without giving it adequate thought and doing your due diligence, in terms of research, on your chosen subject.

To take this a step further, if you want to write about a particular topic that may not have a set market, your book can still sell if you integrate hot topics into the story. Consider the following.

Jane is a sociologist who happens to be a top-class fiction writer, however she's had some difficulty convincing a literary agent that she has enough of a platform to carry a book about the evils of 21st century slavery. So she decided to indie-publish her novel, but chose to create a story centering on female exploitation in Western Africa while placing it within the context of modern day slavery.

Understandably, Jane's book resonated with enough readers to justify a sequel.

Like a painting, the focal point of your story should be a theme that is on people's minds while *your* message provides a suitable frame for that focal point. Remember that most themes are intrinsic; they can be effectively expressed through character growth, dramatic situations and solutions to crises. This gives you the chance to write about what you *want* while still including words that will speak to readers in the metadata.

I've laid a lot of emphasis on this with one goal in mind: metadata and keywords. While I'll discuss this in more detail in the next book in this series, *Write Strategy*, I would like to mention that being able to integrate keywords that reflect trending topics increases the chances of your website coming up in online search engine algorithms. It also increases the odds of your book being found on online retailer websites.

Forethought and planning are key to finding success as an author-entrepreneur. Take this approach and you're one step closer to creating content that sells.

And that's always a good thing!

Takeaway:

1. Don't reinvent the literary wheel. Either write about what's currently trending in society or do research to find out what people are searching for on Google and Amazon.

2. Look at current best-sellers or popular books and write similar content. It may not be what you want to write about but you need to let people know you exist. The sacrifice now can pay off later.

3. Another possibility is to make a trending topic the focal point (painting) of your manuscript set within the frame of your personal message.

Personal Reflection:

1. Go on Twitter or your preferred social media platform. Over the next week observe what people are talking about. Then think: how can these conversations be integrated into my manuscript?

2. If you've already completed your manuscript, think what elements or themes you can write in so that your book is more likely to appear in Amazon or Google searches.

CHAPTER 3

The Writer's Business Plan

Being a successful entrepreneur means that you have a plan. In 2019 I launched a business model that has been well-received by other writerpreneurs. It's called the S.C.A. Model, and I like to say, "reach for the SCAaaa." (Sky? Get it?)

Here's the breakdown: **Strategize, Conceptualize, Analyze**. Each of these terms plays a key part in developing a business plan that will work for you, allowing you to become more competitive in a glutted literary marketplace.

While these terms are pretty self-explanatory, I want you to look at them from a different angle—that of a professional writer.

Before you even put pen to paper or, if you've already completed your piece, before moving forward, stop and consider the following elements. The bullet points beneath each header identify key aspects to the process.

Strategize:

- *What do I WANT to achieve?*

- *What can I REALISTICALLY achieve?*

- *What's my niche/specialty? What do I have to offer in my writing?*

- *Who is my target audience?*

DREAM BIG ... PRACTICALLY.

For the first point, it's great to dream big. Think about what where you want to go and let your writer's imagination run wild.

But the second point (What can I REALISTICALLY achieve) will bring you back to earth. While I hate to burst your bubble, every successful entrepreneur has to have a certain degree of pragmatism.

Keeping a realistic element to your dreams will help you set attainable goals which will, in turn, keep you motivated . So dream big, but dream practically.

IT'S ALL ABOUT YOU ... AND YOUR AUDIENCE

I encourage authors to spend time in self-reflection before they begin writing. The goal is not to figure out your life's purpose but to better understand what exactly your writing has to offer.

Many prospective authors write because they have a message or story to tell. That's fine but *what's in it for your audience?* In the end, it's not what you think about your book but what the reader thinks about the book that drives sales. So before you begin writing, consider what exactly you have to offer that is unique.

Bear in mind, you don't have to be the First Lady to be a successful author. Your uniqueness may come from the fact that you're a master quilter and want to share tips that you've learned along the way. Or perhaps you're a chess guru and want to teach life lessons from the game.

Everyone has something that sets them apart. But before you write it, you need to *find* it. Finding out who you are will also allow you to write with confidence. That confidence will carry over through your work, convincing your audience that you are a person worth listening to. Which leads me to my second point: the audience.

Early in the planning phase of your manuscript, be it fiction or non-fiction, identify who you want to read your book. For some authors, the target audience remains unchanged throughout their entire writing career. For others, like myself, each book or series has a specific audience in mind.

No matter how you do it, be sure that you keep that audience in mind before, during and after the writing process is complete.

Conceptualize:

- *Goal setting*

- *Book writing & production*

- *Beta reviewers*

- *Pre-release marketing*

GOALS ARE WORTH THEIR WEIGHT IN GOLD

...or at least dollar bills! Let's take a closer look at this. By no means do I want to insult your intelligence, but I've discovered it's always helpful to spend a few paragraphs defining the effective goal-setting process.

Let's bring Frank back in on this. About a year after publication, Frank's book has generated a total of 2 sales on KDP. But, instead of getting discouraged, Frank has decided to take a proactive approach to the writing process.

He's decided to start by revamping his manuscript, updating it with new content. Frank has also set a self-imposed deadline to which he's committed. His new file will be available on KDP three weeks after he's set it up.

But instead of waiting for something to happen, he's also set a realistic but ambitious goal of making 50 sales within the next six months.

For Frank that's a huge step forward ... in the right direction.

Goal setting for authors includes writing down— and yes, you *should* write it down— a set number of sales you want to make within a set time frame after publication. Like Frank, make your goal ambitious but practical.

Writer Recap: Dream big but be practical about it.

Keep factors such as potential expos, guest speaking events and online promotions in mind as you plan. Nothing should be done arbitrarily but with careful planning.

Remember, goals are focused, attainable and ambitious while including a set end-date. Without a fixed target date it's just a wish ... not a goal.

BOOK WRITING & PRODUCTION

This is the fun part, the moment of creation. But this part of the process also includes goals. How much will you write each day? When will it be available for critique groups? What is your projected publication date? You've probably heard the semi-funny joke that one eats an elephant "one bite at a time." The point is, sticking to a solid plan will allow you to accomplish big tasks effectively in a minimal amount of time.

As your manuscript starts to shape up, take a small chunk of time each day, say thirty minutes or so, to try and recruit reviewers and beta readers. Try to contact people who work in a field that somehow connects to your book and make connections early, giving reviewers a tentative publication date. If that date changes, keep them posted.

Remember, it's better to overestimate your production time than to underestimate. Most good reviewers have other books on their agenda and nothing sours a relationship like a "missed appointment." If you're indie publishing, give yourself some extra time just in case there are hiccups in the process. If you're traditionally published, the same applies.

While your publisher will probably have a solid reviewer base, you're a key part of the marketing team. So do some legwork, keeping in mind that things don't always go as planned and allowing for a little leeway until the publishing date is set.

Getting honest feedback from beta readers is a vital part of being a successful author. Simply put, beta readers are ordinary people who give you feedback on your complete manuscript. They can help identify plot holes, inconsistencies and even grammar errors.

If you're indie publishing, you definitely want to have them on board as a beta reviewer now can save you negative reviews from the public later.

Carefully curate the feedback you receive from betas, noting which ones give a generally positive opinion of your work. You may want to ask that person to post a review online once the final manuscript has been released. At the same time, cultivate relationships with regular book reviewers so that, once your work is done, you've already created a platform on which you can build a key aspect of your book's success.

But pre-release marketing goes beyond reviewers to actively informing the public about your forthcoming release. I go into marketing steps in the next chapter, but let's lay a foundation right here.

You want to start letting people know about your book at least six months prior to its publication— whether or not you're going the indie route. If you're traditionally published, your publishing company will probably have a variety of marketing tools at its disposal but it never hurts for you to give them a helping hand. After all, the more the merrier, right?

Tell your friends and ask them to tell their other friends. Run pre-release specials on social media, and spend time thinking of out-of-the-box ways to engage the public. If marketing's not your thing, consider hiring a specialist who can help, but be very careful here. Marketing is a bit of a gamble so invest your time and money wisely.

Analyze

Have you ever noticed the "analytics" tab on Twitter? Ever paid attention to the "insights" button on Facebook? How about the flow of traffic to your site as per Google Analytics?

While you may not have spent time poring over the wealth of information available, the fact that we have so many opportunities to analyze our digital impact proves the need for an ongoing, solid analysis of your business plan.

Just about every day of the work week, I spend time analyzing my latest stats on social media and my various websites. I limit my analysis time (no more than 20-30 minutes per day) but this small chunk of my day is positively invaluable.

Why?

Because, like it or not, we are a data-driven society. As a writerpreneur, the plethora of online tools gives you quick, easy ways to figure out what's working ... and what's not. This saves you both time and precious dollars. After all, if a certain advertising platform isn't turning a profit, why bother continuing to invest in it?

Triangulating data from multiple sources allows you to take the analysis step even further. For example, when I want to boost online sales of my books I'll typically use three primary methods to generate online buzz: website promotion, social media and e-mail blasts.

It's best to launch each method at staggered times instead of all at once. By comparing my sales results and/or general online buzz after I announce the promotion on my website but BEFORE I make it public on social media, I can see which method of communication is more effective at this point in the marketing game. What works in June may not work at the end of August when families are going back to school or coming back from trips.

E-mail subscription tools like Mailchimp give valid insight that I can use to corroborate what I'm seeing on Twitter or online sales. The same also applies with e-mail blasts to my subscribers. This data can be compared with the traffic flow data provided by my website host then compared again against the amount of sales reported.

Corroborating the data provided by social media platforms can help you figure out which ads perform best, which method of communication is best for your audience, and what kind of posts or promotions are worth the time and energy.

Having a business plan that doesn't leave time for analysis is like shooting in the dark. You may hit your target some of the time, but you won't most of the time simply because you're not sure what works.

While there are companies that specialize in marketing, the truth is that, with time, patience and creativity, you can achieve success on your own. If you don't have the time, patience or willingness to learn then perhaps considering hiring a marketing specialist may be in your best interest.

But analysis goes beyond the scope of online marketing. You want to also reflect objectively on the offline marketing endeavours you've undertaken. I advocate setting aside at least one hour per month to think about the following:

- What marketing steps have I tried?

- How have I expanded my network or platform?

- What pre-release marketing steps have I taken?

- What has worked or not worked?

- Where can I improve in terms of time management, professional development or honing my writing skills?

Writer's Recap:
Having a business plan that doesn't leave time for analysis is like shooting in the dark.

I want to emphasize the importance of identifying what **works** and what you're doing right in addition to the areas where you need to improve. Writers can often be terrible self-critics but, as an author, you know that there are already enough people out there to criticize your work.

Be your own #1 fan and take some time to reflect on the positive things that have changed, no matter how big or how small.

When analyzing, keep a written log of your thoughts (either digitally or on paper). This will help you ensure that you're not being redundant in your marketing efforts.

It's important not to get stressed out by being a writerpreneur. That basically kills the joy of doing what we do. However, you do want to stay focused and work in a way that makes sense for you. Make your writing fit into your life—don't let it **become** your life.

Don't be discouraged if results aren't where you want them to be. Remember that writing is just one cog in the machine of being a successful writerpreneur. There are a lot of other factors to consider, most of which take time to achieve.

Determination, commitment to your writing business and a detailed analysis can help you get to where you want to be.

Takeaway:

- Everything begins with a plan. Follow the SCA model as you develop your own growth strategy. **Strategize. Conceptualize. Analyze.**

- Strategize is the actual planning. It involves figuring out what you're going to do and why you're in a position to do it.

- Conceptualizes entails active goal-setting. You've figured out what you want to achieve, now you're deciding how you're going to do it. In this stage, you create your book and initiate pre-release marketing.

- Analyze is an ongoing process. In this stage, you identify both the strengths and weaknesses of your marketing strategy and the product itself. You should spend a little time each day analyzing data if your schedule allows but make it a point to at least have a "self-check-in" on a monthly basis.

- Be sure to note what you're doing right as well as where you need to improve. Being your own #1 fan will help keep you motivated.

Personal Reflection

1. Write out your own business plan based on the materials and resources provided above.

2. Identify 3 possible beta-readers for your next manuscript or a current manuscript. Contact them and make your expectations clear.

3. Set a schedule for your analysis time while refusing to allow it to degenerate into a time-vampire. Remember fit your writing into your life. Don't let it become your life.

CHAPTER 4:

The Marketing Machine

I want you to close your eyes for a minute and picture a machine. That's right, go ahead. Put the book down and just picture any kind of machine. Car, tractor, doesn't matter. Big, small, or in the middle. Mine is blue with a kind of shovel-like thing in the front. Don't ask me why the shovel. It's just there.

Okay, now after you've opened your eyes, imagine you're standing in front of the machine's engine and there are all kinds of gears that grind and belts that whir. It all has to come together to make a functioning product—a product that will get top reviews, win awards and have some machine enthusiasts telling their friends on Facebook that they absolutely MUST get this machine too.

I'm sure you see where I'm going with this. Writing is just one cog in the machine. Yes, you should have awesome content but, the truth is, you'll continue to grow as an author and everyone's got to start some-where. So what have successful authors learned?

If good content is a cog in the machine, then good marketing is its key.

I've spent a good number of hours researching the habits of some very successful authors—authors who have literally earned millions on various platforms. While I can't guarantee anyone's success, there are several key habits that these authors maintain which clearly have a bearing on their overall performance.

Let's take a look. For privacy purposes, I've altered the identity of these authors, some of whom started off self-publishing their works.

Jane committed early in her writing career to setting aside 4 hours per day for writing. She backs that up with frequent targeted public speaking which, of course, brings her into contact with her prime audience on a regular basis. In addition, she makes sure that her content is appealing—its look, the actual story, everything is carefully created with her target audience in mind.

Luke goes above and beyond to make his charac-ters real to his audience. He began by writing about issues that he feels are underrepresented. By creating fictional characters that appealed to his audience and reflected changing social attitudes, he won them to his stories.

Then Luke implemented simple, effective and original ways of getting his readers to engage with his fictitious characters beyond the book. He sought reader feedback on a per-chapter basis, learning what his audience liked while in the trenches.

Steve leveraged the power of an online social media platform, turning free tools like Facebook to his advantage. While many authors recognize the power of social media, Steve focused on having *engaged* followers instead of simply just having followers. I recently interviewed him and found that he still feels a need to improve his skills in building a "community of readers."

Writer's Recap:
Writing is just one cog in a big machine. It takes time to get the results you may want.

Keeping readers engaged gave him an audience that was ready to snap up his next book. In addition, Steve focused primarily upon e-books, making sure that his products were easily accessible to his audience.

Finally, he made *himself* available. By that I mean that the pictures he posted were unedited, unprofessional and totally personal. While this may seem strange and, perhaps a little creepy if you're not into the whole social media craze, readers **love it** when authors post everyday pictures of themselves and their families.

Perhaps because our world features so many "picture-perfect" moments, we've actually come to the point that ordinary impressions appeal to us. It makes sense, in a way. After all, if the author is more relatable then perhaps so are his books.

The 4CM Method

The main elements that contributed to the success of these authors can be simplified to the following, what I call the 4CM method. While each element can technically be considered different aspects of marketing, I've placed marketing into its own category because I plan to spend a good bit of time on it over the next two chapters. So here is the 4CM method:

- Commitment

- Community

- Content

- Conferences

- Marketing

Each of these is a valuable tool in the writerpreneur toolkit, but not all of them will work for you. That's why you need to capitalize on your strengths, using them to compensate for those areas in which you struggle.

Let's zero in on this.

We've already covered *commitment* in our segment on the "Write Mentality" so I won't belabor the point. Rather let's focus on the other aspects of 4CM that can really make a difference.

Community

Helen Keller is quoted as saying, "Alone, we can do so little; together, we can do so much." This is true in a variety of circumstances; it's especially true in writing.

As an entrepreneur you need to cultivate the idea of a community—in every sense of the word. Your clients (readers) are an essential part of your community, not only because they can drive current sales, but also because they are the ones that are impacting future sales based on their reviews and their decision to talk (or not talk) to their friends about your latest book.

Beyond direct sales, readers offer insight into the topics that are of interest to society as a whole. It's a potential loop. Cultivating a sense of community can result in more compelling writing that resonates with more readers which can ultimately create a stronger community of readers.

To piggyback off that thought, a community of readers can give you quick feedback on your current work-in-progress. While your publisher may not want that information released to the public, if you're indie-publishing, you're in control. How much or how little you share is up to you. A reader community is an awesome way to hook potential fans while minimizing the risk of potentially devastating reviews.

So how do you create a community after you've gotten your book out there? Take the following steps:

Show readers they're valued. Like any other customer, readers want to know that they matter. Turn that desire into an opportunity to make a personable connection.

1. Respond to e-mails and messages from readers

2. Tweet occasional appreciation messages

3. Reward loyal followers with freebies monthly

4. Post appropriate pictures of yourself with readers. Be sure to get their consent first.

Nurturing the idea and feeling of community is an ongoing process. Subscribe to my writerpreneur e-mail list on my website, **JPRobinsonBooks.com**, for free community building tips, marketing strategies and more.

Show readers you listen. Engage and involve them with the actual writing process. Here's how:

1. Ask them for character name suggestions

2. Ask their opinion when you've got a plot problem

3. Hold a survey about cover preference

4. Respond to feedback (positive or negative) in a courteous and appreciate manner

Content

This is the part where talent gets to shine. Without a doubt, every good writer has got to have stellar content. Grammar can be corrected and punctuation can be improved, but the content is the soul of a story —and that can't be corrected by spell check.

Give your book the edge by weaving a story that will hook reader's emotions, a story that is relatable and engaging. If you need tips on that, the first book in this series, *Write History*, give solid strategies for creating 3D characters.

Try your story idea out with peer review groups, talk about it with trusted family or friends and see how they respond. Write your idea down, then don't think about it for a few weeks. Go back to it later and see if you still feel the same urgency, the same willingness to commit precious hours of your life to that manuscript. If not, then perhaps it's not a story you need to write ... yet.

To give your inner muse some caffeine, consider taking the following steps after identifying your TA (target audience).

1. Meet with members of that group and interview them. Focus on their interests and challenges.

2. Look at social issues and meet with people who have been affected by both sides of the problem. Hear their stories.

3. People-watch. Stories are nurtured in the womb of observation.

4. Reflect on your interests and see if they can be meshed with trending themes.

Conferences

Good conferences are like caffeine—both are an essential part of a writer's well-being. Whether you participate as a speaker or an attendee, conferences enable you to engage with readers and authors in a dynamic and educational way.

Writer's Recap:
Show readers that they're valued
and that you listen to them.

If you're not into public speaking, ask the organizer for permission to bring along previously published titles or an opportunity to display a size-appropriate banner to your website.

Alternatively, you can reach out a few months before the event and offer to post a link to their website on your own website. Encourage the event host to do the same. Not only can this drive more traffic to your site, it can also raise your ranking on major search engines such as Google.

If you're into public speaking, you have an additional advantage. Connect with conference leaders and see if you'd be a good fit for their portfolio.

It's important to note that conferences don't have to be large-scale events. For our purposes, a "conference" may well be a public engagement event in which you and others play a part. Think book-signing or even a local writing club meeting here.

Consider the following:

1. Connect with local charitable causes that you're passionate about or a hospital to which you have a personal connection. Organize an event in which you speak then sell books while giving a portion of those proceeds to the institution. Not only is this good publicity, but it allows you to support meaningful change in your community.

2. A read-aloud to children (assuming your book is age-appropriate) or to another gathering of your target audience.

Marketing

At this point you may be tempted to put down this book, throw up your hands and say, "I don't have time for this! Why even bother to spend so much time marketing?"

In reply, I'd point you to rather chilling data collected by the Washington Post. In 2017, only 19% of Americans indicated that they read for personal interest on a typical day.[2] In a 2019 report, the Post cited that "the average American spent as little as 15 minutes reading for pleasure."[3] Need I say that screen time has increased dramatically?

The point is, the number of active readers in the United States is rapidly declining. While it is true that the market is now global and authors have unprecedented abilities to conduct sales on an international scale, the odds are that most of your sales will come from readers in the United States. And, given the data, it is clear that the number of available *readers* in the national pool is shrinking.

---

2 (Ingraham, 2018)

3 (Ingraham, 2019)

In order to reach and engage that audience, you will need to put time, energy and money into marketing. Hopefully as little as possible.

I often hear authors state that they apply marketing techniques and I can't help but wonder if they realize just how many components come together to making a successful sale. Marketing is a lot more than giving someone money and hoping for results or asking people you know to buy your book.

Marketing is a game with shifting pieces, changing rules and fluid dynamics.

To lay the background for where we're going, let's mentally compare marketing to walking into an airport and buying a plane ticket. Now, I realize that most of us book tickets online or on the phone, but just walk with me here.

So, you're in this airport and there are tons of planes all around you, any of which could, potentially, take you to your destination. After all, a plane's a plane, right?

But you have a set destination in mind (remember my section on strategizing?) and, as such, you realize that there are a limited number of flights that can get you where you want to go. With that thought, you've unconsciously narrowed your possible flight options from a hundred to a few dozen.

Great job, however you can only board *one* plane.

So now you consider other factors. Factors such as departure time, flight length, number of stops and, of course, cost. Ultimately you make your choice when all the factors line up in a way that makes sense to you.

Now let's swing this into marketing your book. The parallel is pretty straightforward but, at the risk of insulting your intelligence, let me just point out a few critical elements.

Marketing is a means to an end—a plane to get you somewhere. Unless you get on that plane you'll go nowhere beyond where your own two legs can carry you. And that's probably not as far as you want to go. Metaphorically speaking, your book's ability to go places is limited without a solid marketing plan.

There are a ton of different marketing avenues you can pursue, just like there are a lot of planes in an airport. But you need to choose one general approach at a time. Yes, you'll sometimes need to stop "mid-flight" and alter course, just like you may need to transfer mid-flight to another airplane. No matter what happens, keep it organized and focused so you're better able to identify what works from what doesn't work.

There's always an element of risk. We don't like to think about it, but there's always an unfortunate amount of risk involved with boarding a plane. Things don't always go as planned. It's important to recognize the risk when investing your money and also to minimize the risk by doing field research, checking out a company's reviews and also minimizing your investment until you see proven, data-driven results.

Remember that turbulence can happen at any time. By that I mean market volatility, sports events and unpredictable events such as natural disasters, which will result in more people are focusing on their TV screens instead of books. While you should recognize the risk, don't let it make you afraid to get on board.

You've gotta find the right plane. You need to find a marketing mix that will let you achieve the goal you set back in Chapter 3. Compare the various factors in your marketing plan (time commitment, feasibility, cost etc...) and *get on board*. Narrow your options to the two or three that are most likely to succeed. Don't risk too much at once. Again, remember that things can always go wrong (yes, I know I'm being quite the optimist here) and you want to avoid making legal commitments that will hurt you now or in the future.

So you've made your decision, got on the plane and arrived at your destination without mishap. But this flight is only good for today. There will come another time when you must make another journey to another destination.

Perhaps it will be a place much further than where you are right now. Then the process begins all over again. But the cost will be higher, the risk will be greater and the reward will be sweeter.

So how do you optimize your chances at success?

Buckle on your seat belt. You're about to find out.

Takeaway:

1. Writing is just one cog in the writerpreneur machine. Successful marketing is its key.
2. The 4CM model identifies key characteristics of successful authors: commitment, community, content, conferences and marketing.
3. As the number of readers in the United States continues to decline, effective marketing strategies become more needful.
4. Effective marketing can be compared to purchasing a ticket at an airport. A variety of factors must be considered before committing.

Personal Reflection:

1. Again, focus on a current or previously published manuscript. How can it fit into the 4CM model?
2. Diagram your plans to use the 4CM model in the chart below. Use a separate piece of paper for more space. I've excluded commitment here because we've explored it in an earlier chapter.

	build a community by...	
I plan to...	improve my content by...	
	attend ____ conference	
	think about ____ marketing strategy	

CHAPTER 5:

Fix the Mix

Have you ever made brownies? The store-bought stuff, not the really good kind that you make from scratch. Well, if you have, you'll realize there's a precise formula you need to follow to get that perfect gooey consistency that just lets the chocolate melt inside your mouth, giving your taste buds every reason to celebrate.

Okay, I better stop or the scale will hate me when I step on it tomorrow. My point in mentioning that there's a certain amount of eggs, water and whatever else you put in the mixing bowl is straightforward. It's a mix. A guided formula that brings predictable (but not guaranteed) results. Hey, those guys will even tell you how long to bake the brownies for optimal results.

Well, in like manner, we in the marketing field have pre-programmed ingredients that fall into something we call the "marketing mix." In general terms, the marketing mix is what a business does to promote its product.

Now I'm going to avoid getting all techie but I am going to use some marketing terminology. If you feel overwhelmed at all, or just need a quick refresher, there's a short glossary at the end of this book that contains some of the most important terms.

Today we'll focus on two major aspects of a typical marketing mix: the STP process and the 4Ps. Both are models that help marketers better conceptualize the buyer/seller relationship and help us better answer the critical question: *how can I increase sales?*

The fundamental economic problem is that we have unlimited wants with limited resources. This carries over into advertising as we all have limited budgets but want unlimited sales. The STP process and 4Ps, when applied to a writing business, can help you stretch your dollars and make solid business decisions.

For writers, this doesn't need to be complex. But if you're wondering why sales don't seem to be what they should, I'd encourage you to "fix the mix."

Let's look at the first of the two major ingredients: The STP process.

STP for writers

STP, or Segmentation, Targeting and Positioning, is one of the most common ways of illustrating the concept of marketing.

Segmentation:

Marketing techniques have radically changed over the past seventy years, as has our understanding of human purchasing behavior. In the early years of television, advertisers simply blasted their message out to the masses while hoping to get the interest of a few viewers.

Then came the rise of mail and catalogue advertising which allowed for more focused (segmented) marketing based on the content of the catalogue. *Field and Stream* is not likely to advertise high-heeled shoes because they aren't suited to their target audience. Now, however, with the rise of online advertising platforms such as those offered by Facebook, Google and others, marketers are able to reach individual consumers with ads based on the consumer's interests and prior browsing history.

No book was written for everyone. No *product* was made for everyone. Successful writerpreneurs recognize this and, as such, write for specific chunks of the reader market. You need to identify what segments of the market will be most likely to give you a return on your investment based on their similarities and their differences.

You can do this simply by thinking about the messages, or themes, in your book. Who is most likely to be interested in it? Why?

To give a realistic example, when writing my novel *In the Shadow of Your Wings,* I decided to analyze the reader market based on psychographic and demographic characteristics. Basically that's a fancy way of saying I made my determination based on the things they like to read and their gender.

I felt it was a story that would appeal mostly to female readers in the Christian market but had messages that would also appeal to parents. Finally, my third segment was libraries or institutions servicing a body of inspirational fiction readers.

Writer's Recap:
Two fundamental marketing models you should know are the STP process and the 4Ps. Both can help you market effectively.

So, from an entirely nebulous market of potential readers, I narrowed it down to three segments of the reader market:

1. Female readers interested in Christian fiction

2. Parents looking for an encouraging message

3. Libraries/institutions with a large inspirational fiction readership

Why do this? Because, since no product is perfect for everyone, your marketing dollars will be better spent if you are using them to get your message in front of people who are more likely to be interested in it.

Think back to our plane analogy. You have to know where you want to go before you purchase a ticket. If you want to fly to Paris, it's unlikely you'll choose a direct flight to Sydney. Your personal interests lead you to focus on a particular segment of available flight options—those bound for Paris.

Targeting

Once you've identified the segments of the market that are most likely to be interested in your product, you need to move on to decide which segment to "target." By this, I mean the segment of the market to which you're going to advertise your book.

The essential question of the "T" part in STP is *who will give me the best ROI?* You want to keep the following in mind as you select your target group:

1. Think overall profitability not just the size of the group.

2. Who is prepared to pay what you want for your book? Why will the pay it?

3. Can you affordably REACH that segment of the market?

Keep in mind that this step is where you identify your "target" marketing audience. This can change, depending on the strategy you're planning to employ and what's going on in society at the time.

For example, if World Senior Citizen's Day is coming up and you've written a book on how senior citizens can lead a successful, fulfilled life while dealing with Alzheimer's disease, you may want to target a different segment of the market than you would on Mother's Day or Father's Day.

On World Senior Citizen's Day, you may want to target senior citizens directly—while of course running a promotion that makes your book affordable for people on a fixed income—but on Mother/Father's Day, you want to target the adult *children* of senior citizens who may have a parent that is battling Alzheimer's disease. Your target is different because of changing dynamics in the market.

Let me go bring back my example with *In the Shadow of Your Wings.* Out of my three segments, in my initial marketing strategy, I recognized that the segment I wanted to target was that of females interested in Christian fiction.

Why?

Because, while individual libraries and parents are both tempting marketing targets, they are less likely to give me the return on my investment. Again, that can change depending on trends in the market and a variety of factors but, for this particular marketing strategy, my first segment is the one to target.

Positioning your offer

This is where you get to unleash your writer's creativity. Positioning comes down to one question: *how will consumers know your product exists?*

Keep in mind that an estimated million books are self-published every year[4] in addition to the titles released by traditional publishers. Add to that the decreasing numbers of readers I referenced earlier and you'll see why having a good position is vital to the mix. **Consider the following as you develop your marketing strategy:**

1. What marketing channels will you use or does your publisher already use? (I.E. websites, bookstores, retail chains)

2. What endorsements can you acquire? How will you use positive book reviews?

3. Does your book reflect a professional layout in its cover, typesetting and editing? How can you capitalize on this?

Don't be discouraged if you can't answer many of these questions. The STP process for writers is effective and can help you narrow the gap between where you are and where you want to go. It's an ongoing process that can challenge the best of us at times.

---

4 **Publishers Weekly (2017)**

But placing your book in front of the right people with the right message at the right time will lead to an increase in sales. That's STP in action.

By segmenting the market, knowing which group you want to target via your current marketing strategy, and positioning your product so it can get the attention it deserves, you're well on your way to making awesome brownies—erm, sales!

The 4Ps:

The second ingredient in the marketing mix is called the 4Ps: *product, price, place, promotion.* These four elements are so important that sometimes the 4Ps are referred to as the marketing mix by themselves.

To a certain degree this overlaps with the STP process but it's important for you as a writerpreneur to understand each marketing model and decide how to make it work for you. Here's the magic formula:

The right product at the right price in the right place with the right promotion. That pretty much guarantees a sale. Now you see why marketing is a combination of science and art?

That doesn't mean it has to be complex. I hope my approach below can give you a framework to easily find the right mix.

Product: *Are people curious about your book's topic?*

Price: *Is the book priced high enough to give you a profit but low enough to be affordable?*

Place: *Is your book in an environment that will let it shine?*

Promotion: *What specials/discounts/advertising methods will you use? How will you diversify them? How long will they run?*

These are all questions that you need to answer before and during the "life cycle" of your book. The good news is that nothing with marketing is ever set in stone. There is always room to stop, take a deep breath, and figure out where you're going from here.

The 4Ps in action

In this section, I'm going to take the 4Ps and use them to model the development of a marketing strategy that targets a key component of successful authors that we've already identified: **building a community of readers.** Obviously the more people out there that read your book, the more likely you are to grow an online following. But that isn't always the case.

I've known award-winning authors that struggled to grow and keep those Twitter numbers cranking. And what if you're an indie-author, now trying to get your name out there? The information below can let you approach this vital aspect of marketing with confidence. Use the information as a guide to get you started on your own marketing plan or just keep it for quick reference.

Let's do this.

Setting: Imagine you currently have a combined social media following of 500 people but you know you need more. You've also noticed that they're not too engaged. On average you see only 15 out of the 500 respond to your posts.

Goal: To increase the NUMBER of your social media followers by 10 percent within the next 90 days.

Even though you know that the engagement level of your followers is something you want to improve, it's best to focus on one aspect of your writing business at a time so you don't feel overwhelmed. After all, you've got a job, possibly a family, and a million other things competing for your time.

Be effective and focus. Your stress-level (and your hair) will thank you.

So now that you've given yourself a reasonable goal with a set deadline, I'm ready to throw the 4Ps out there. Keep in mind that the ultimate goal of the

4Ps is to result in a sale. So, while your short-term goal is to increase your follower count, if the mix is just right, you'll also get some money in your bank account.

PRODUCT:

Your book is your product so the community you build should revolve around your writing. Do this by taking the following steps:

Focused blogging: Your blog should only be about your writing. While you may have guest posts and have personal pictures on occasion, by and large, your blog needs to have ONE focus.

This way you automatically cultivate a community that's interested in your product. You are segmenting the market of available bloggers, wooing in those who are most likely to make a purchase.

Manuscript Tidbits: Share snippets of your WIP, allow people to comment and give feedback (see Chapter 5 notes on community building strategies). Also blog about the challenges you face when writing the manuscript, especially if they are emotional challenges that can resonate with your audience.

PRICE:

If the price isn't right, your product will either be undervalued or under-appreciated. Glean information while building reader relations by:

Surveys: Most social media platforms allow users to conduct polls, so survey your followers about the appropriate price for a product. How much should an e-book cost? A paperback?

Online conversations: Tweet about the cost of books you've purchased, the value for the money etc... Most people like to share their opinions about products so ask and you will get feedback.

Be sure to direct the conversation so it revolves around books that are comparable to yours but aren't yours. That way you don't attract negative attention to your product but gain critical insight while deflecting possible negative attention elsewhere.

As you start to have open conversations you build those critical relationships that can turn a social media user into a follower, and a follower into a customer.

PLACE:

Once you have a high-quality product, you can leverage its attractive features to grow your product's following. But, like a diamond, it is critical that your product (your book) is displayed in a way that will allow its beauty to be seen. Let's start with the obvious:

Your website: Websites can be a real deterrent from a sale. If the site is cluttered or if the information can't be easily found and purchased, you can easily turn off followers and customers. Have you ever noticed how Amazon throws products right in your face? And that handy little "Buy-with-1-click" button?

We like things to be convenient. ***So make it easy for people to find your latest titles on your website.*** A few days before I embarked in a major marketing campaign in 2019, I gave my site a complete overhaul. While I don't think you can read the text, I'm throwing in a screenshot:

The main thing I'd like you to notice here is how easy it is to make a purchase. There's nothing hidden, and I'm not making the potential reader dig for information. Everything is accessible and all he or she needs to do … is click on their favorite retailer's icon.

When designing your website, be sure that the most relevant information is up front: your newest release, a big announcement, whatever it is that you want consumers to know right away. Remember, you're competing with their e-mail, smart phone, people in the room and a million other distractions. You've only got their attention for a few precious seconds. So, make them count.

You're competing with ... a million
other distractions for their attention
So, make them count.

Group/reader social media pages: I interviewed a NYT bestselling author whose books outsold JK Rowling and Stephen King at one time. One of my questions, predictably, revolved around marketing. I wanted to know what community-building techniques this guy implemented.

Now, of course there are a variety of factors that contribute to an author's success. As I said before, there is no genie-in-the-lamp when it comes to selling your book. But this author's response was surprising because it emphasized an area of marketing whose value I had previously underestimated: group and reader social media pages.

It goes without saying that, as an author, you need to have a social media presence. But it's also important to use your social media time as a means of becoming involved with reader pages that feature your genre. You also want to cultivate the relationships you grow on other pages so that you readers' loyalty to your "brand" will spill over into your next book release.

PROMOTION:

I want to make a confession.

I once ran a marketing campaign ... that failed. Abysmally. Totally.

Was it expensive?

Yes.

Was it worth it?

Totally.

Would I do it again?

Absolutely, but with some modifications.

I wanted to run a campaign in a specific community. So I got in touch with my contacts and set this thing up. Ads were designed, everything queued up and they went live.

Nothing.

Not one response. Not one click. Not even one!

There was absolutely nothing that any of my data-analysis tools could attribute to my campaign. Okay, so halfway through the campaign I saw a little traction, but it was nothing like I had envisioned.

And I was crushed.

But then my inner marketing muse started analyzing the situation from a professional standpoint. I've attracted attendees to high-profile galas in New York city. I've convinced people to donate thousands to various causes. I'm pretty confident that I know how to drive traffic to a website.

So, *what did I do wrong?*

Ultimately I realized that my promotion was not appropriate for the neighborhood's demographics. Simply put, I had placed a very compelling ad targeting readers in an area in which there aren't a lot of readers.

Not too smart, huh? Yeah. I agree. Chalk that up to a reminder that we all make mistakes.

But, on the bright side, the fiasco gave me a real-life scenario to prove that the promotion (or the way you let customers know about your product) has to be relevant to *them*. You want to know the area in which you're going to promote your product. To give a non-literary example, would it make sense for a company specializing in high-calorie beverages to advertise in a very health-conscious neighborhood?

Not unless they're rolling out a zero-calorie option. While this is essentially common sense, it's easy to miss if you're caught up in the beauty of your book and don't step back and objectively look at the situation.

Not only must your product be relevant to the consumer, but your method of delivery and the location in which it is promoted should also resonate.

Keep the following in mind:

1. Have a simple ad design

2. Choose the method of promotion most likely to generate a good ROI

3. Keep your target group in mind when designing your ad

4. Choose a promotion method that will best capture the attention of your target group

5. Be sure to promote it in a place where your target group is MOST LIKELY to see it

Whether you're using Facebook Ads or YouTube, be sure that your promotion is visible to the group you want to hit.

So, after applying these strategies, you're in a position where you can analyze the data and see if you have achieved your objective. If you have, that's awesome! You're ready to move on to your second goal of increasing follower engagement.

If not, now is the time to sit back and decide what other route you want to pursue before moving on to another goal.

Takeaway:

1. The STP Process and 4Ps can help you understand how to effectively market.

2. By segmenting the market you can save valuable dollars and target readers who are more likely to buy your book (product).

3. Be sure you're thinking of the readers when you design and promote your product.

Personal reflection:

1. Choose a personal goal and develop a plan using the 4Ps.

2. Take your current WIP or a previous manuscript. Run it through the STP process. What segment of the market are you targeting? How will you position your offer?

CHAPTER 6

The Write Thing at the Write Time

As with anything else, the most effective way to balance the different demands upon authors is to have a schedule. When it comes to carving out a niche in the writing world, be prepared to have years of your life available.

Sounds depressing?

I don't mean for it to be!

I advocate dividing your year into quarters with each three-month period focusing on a specific segment of your proposed marketing mix. Each month within that quarter should, in turn, have different strategies employed.

Q1	Q2	Q3	Q4
BLOGGING	ENGAGING READERS	SOCIAL MEDIA	PUBLIC EVENTS

Using a spreadsheet or paper chart, document the following:

- Your quarterly focus
- The steps employed and the frequency with which you employed them
- The results you've seen
- Suggestions for improvement.

In our chart above, you can see how the year is easily broken down with a different goal being the focus of each quarter. While I didn't illustrate a strategy for each month, every thirty days you want to try a different approach to achieve the same end-goal.

For example, if I'm working on public events in quarter 4, then each month I want to either set up a public speaking event or actively host a public speaking event.

It is best to plan your year out in advance, working around personal commitments and unimportant things like a full-time job! If your personal schedule won't allow you to have a different focus-area per quarter, consider working on the same area for two quarters instead of just one.

The key is to continuously grow in a low-stress, organized manner, varying your approach while giving yourself time to learn new skills. In the next book in this series, *Write Strategy*, I will go further into the marketing world and identify time-saving, budget-friendly ways to engage readers, build your social media following, and collaborate effectively.

Always remember that this is a flexible model. If a strategy you're employing works one month, try it again the next month. Conversely, if you are certain that your current strategy isn't going to work out, don't feel pressured to stick it out the full thirty days.

Remember, as a writerpreneur you must continue to hone your writing *and* entrepreneur skills but at a pace that works best for you, taking your personal obligations into account. After all, if you won't enjoy the journey ... why take it?

Although it may take time to bring your plans to fruition, the progress you make can increase your drive to succeed and keep you motivated.

Takeaway:

1. Divide your year into quarters then into months.

2. Give each quarter a different focus and each month employ a different strategy.

3. Keep careful records, along with strategies to improve, so you can plan more effectively.

Personal reflection:

Using the chart outlined above, create your own plan for next year. Divide it by quarters and then by months in a way that works best with your schedule. Feel free to adapt it at any time.

A note from the author

In terms of writing, the best advice I've ever heard came from a fellow author. She said, "Enjoy the journey." Over the years, I've brooded on those three words, extracting layers of meaning from their literary depths. Writing is a journey, one that changes us each time we write.

As emerging technologies continue to shape the publishing world, it will become even more essential for everyone in the professional writing industry to continue to learn and grow. But, not only is writing a journey, it is one that we are meant to enjoy. Whether we're creating worlds, rehearsing powerful memories or sharing knowledge, every word we craft is another step on that road.

To that end, I continue to offer individualized services to authors, such as manuscript critiques, data-driven, interactive writing workshops and writing resources on my website: **www. JPRobinsonBooks.com.**

The content I've shared here may seem daunting, but apply it in stages, always remembering that marketing and sales are, like writing itself, all stages of the journey. While writing is, to a certain degree, an individualized profession, none of us can succeed alone.

I'd love to hear about your writing journey, so stay connected on Facebook and Twitter (@JPRobinsonBooks).

Enjoy the journey,

JP Robinson

Glossary of terms

Barrier to entry-start-up costs or other obstacles that prevent someone from starting a business

Beta readers- readers who give you valid feedback on your plot during or just after the manuscript is written and prior to publication. They're a sounding board.

Four (4)Ps- The typical variables of a standard marketing mix. Product, price, place, promotion.

Indie/Self-publishing- Publishing a book by yourself or paying someone to publish it for you.

Marketing mix-the variables you employ to get your book sold

Metadata-data that gives information about your book so it can be more easily found (talk about this more) along with keywords

Return on Investment-ROI is the what you get out of your investment, taking into account what you've put in. A high ROI is a good thing.

STP Process-standard marketing procedure. Segmentation, targeting, positioning an offer.

Traditional publishing-a publisher handles all costs and most/all aspects of publication. The author is paid a royalty on copies sold.

Writerpreneur-an author who considers writing to be a business.

Works referenced

Ingraham, Christopher. "Leisure Reading in the U.S. Is at an All-time Low." The Washington Post. June 29, 2018. Accessed July 06, 2019. https://www.washingtonpost.com/news/wonk/wp/2018/06/29/leisure-reading-in-the-u-s-is-at-an-all-time-low/?utm_term=.414f632bdb54.

Ingraham, Christopher. "Screen Time Is Rising, Reading Is Falling, and It's Not Young People's Fault." The Washington Post. June 21, 2019. Accessed July 06, 2019. https://www.washingtonpost.com/business/2019/06/21/screen-time-is-rising-reading-is-falling-its-not-young-peoples-fault/?utm_term=.3fcb942f66b7.

Milliot, Jim. "The Number of Self-Published Titles Cracked 1 Million in 2017." PublishersWeekly.com. October 10, 2018. Accessed July 06, 2019. https://www.publishersweekly.com/pw/by-topic/industry-news/publisher-news/article/78291-the-number-of-self-published-titles-cracked-1-million-in-2017.html.

Other books in the series: *Workshop-in-your-pocket*

- **Write History:** Establish compelling settings, create authentic 3D historical characters, hook reader emotions and more.

- **Write Strategy (available in 2020):** Backed by data and interviews with some of today's most successful authors, *Write Strategy* teaches cost-effective strategies to market, promote and sell your book.

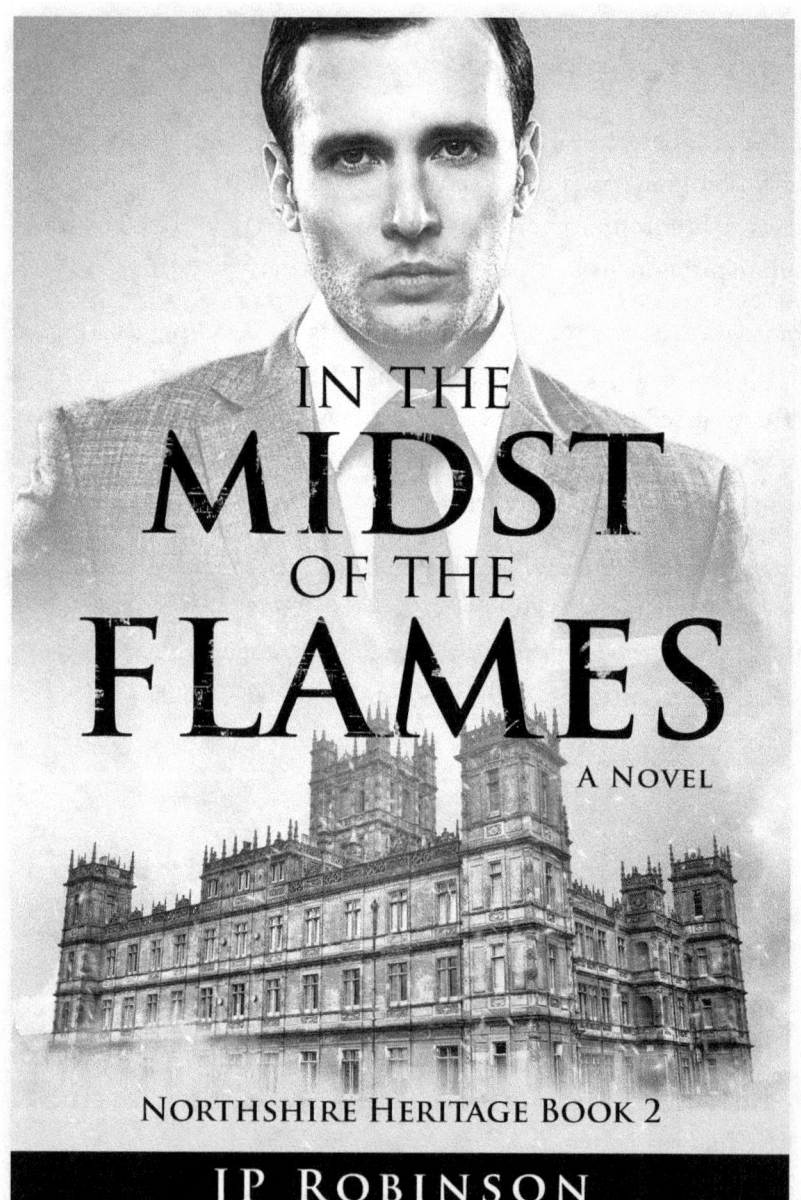

IN THE
MIDST
OF THE
FLAMES

A NOVEL

NORTHSHIRE HERITAGE BOOK 2

JP ROBINSON

In the Midst of the Flames (Northshire Heritage II)

Europe is burning.

As the fires of the Great War rage across the continent, both the Steele and Thompson families are caught in the midst of the inferno.

Malcolm must face the consequences of his betrayal as he begins the long journey home while Leila's secret past threatens the future of Northshire Estate … and her marriage.

Following Will's capture by the Germans, he encounters challenges on a new front—that of the heart—while Eleanor, learning her husband is still alive, goes to the heat of the war zone, hoping to find him.

Thomas risks everything in a high-stakes political gamble, bringing Britain to the brink of obliteration as Robert Hughes struggles to orchestrate his downfall.

Will everything be reduced to ashes? Or does God still walk with those who, through faith, step out into the midst of the flames?

Buy your copy today.
JPRobinsonBooks.com

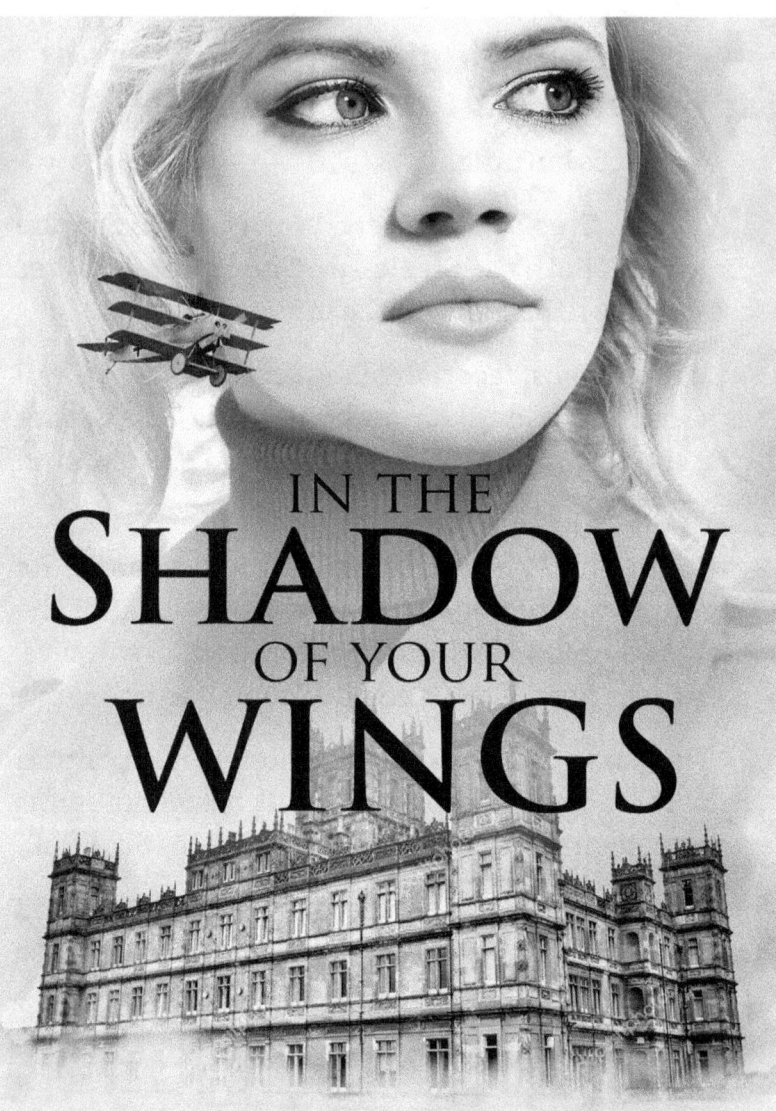

IN THE
SHADOW
OF YOUR
WINGS

NORTHSHIRE HERITAGE BOOK 1

JP ROBINSON

In the Shadow of Your Wings (Northshire Heritage I)

Leila Durand, an elite German spy charged with infiltrating the home of British icon Thomas Steele, sees the war as a chance to move beyond the pain of st. But everything changes when she falls in love with Thomas's son, Malcolm. Is there a way to reconcile her love for Germany and her love for the enemy?

Thomas Steele sees the war as an opportunity for his profligate son, Malcolm, to find a purpose greater than himself. But when Malcolm rebels, it falls to Thomas to make tough decisions.

The war's reach extends to the heart. Eleanor Thompson finds her faith is pushed to the breaking point when her husband disappears on the battle front and her daughter is killed in a German air raid. Where is God in the midst of her pain?

In the Shadow of Your Wings presents inescapable truth that resonates across the past century. Then as now, the struggle for faith is real. Then as now, there is a refuge for all who will come beneath the shadow of God's wings.

Buy your copy today.
JPRobinsonBooks.com

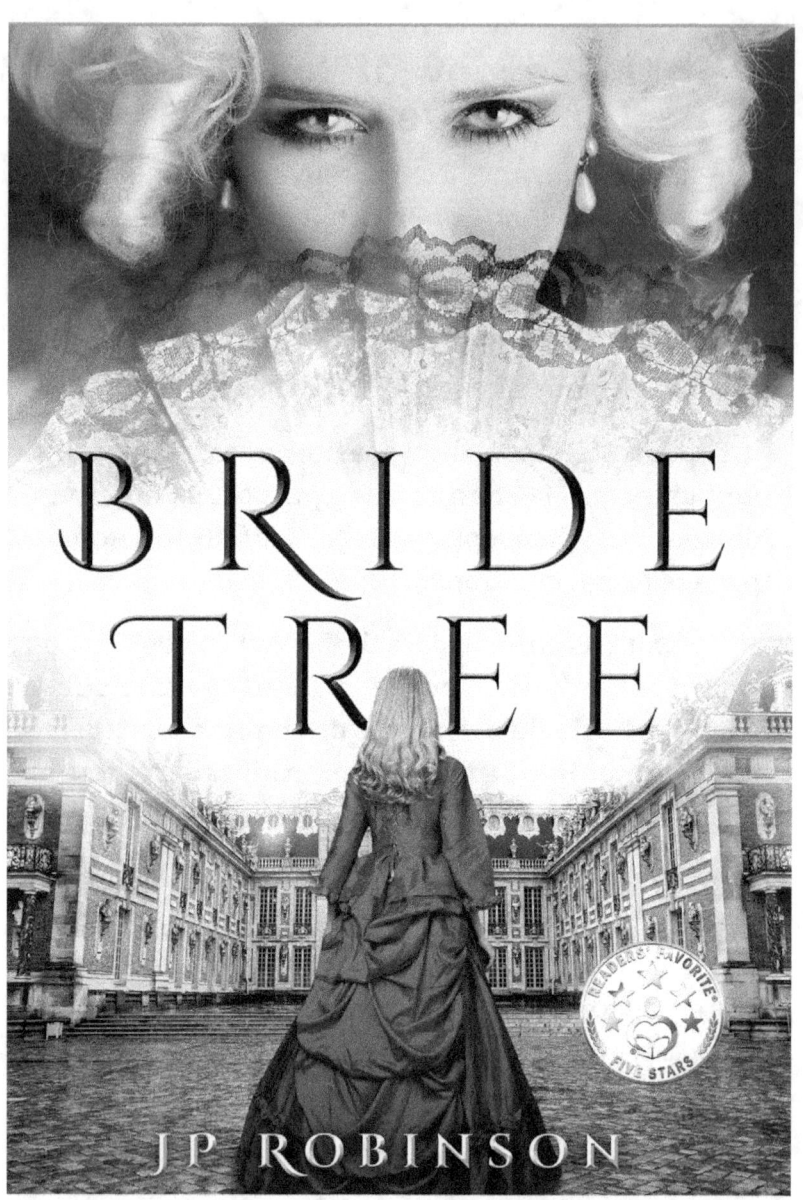

BRIDE TREE

JP ROBINSON

SECRETS OF VERSAILLES II

Bride Tree
(Secrets of Versailles II)

UNMASK THE TRUTH

Bride Tree, a sweeping allegory of the Church set in the tumultuous French Revolution era, fuses alternative history with romantic suspense.

The year is 1789. France is reeling under the impact of a civil war between its social classes. When a secret agent from Rome joins forces with a vindictive politician bent on revenge, the stage is set for an explosive outcome that will shake the country to its core.

Meanwhile, Queen Marie-Antoinette engages the help of her lady-in-waiting, Viviane de Lussan, in a desperate battle to keep her throne… and her head. But how can she win a struggle she seems fated to lose?

Amid the chaos of the revolution, Viviane's heart is torn between a nobleman who sacrifices everything for her and a peasant who promises true freedom.

Buy your copy today.
JPRobinsonBooks.com

JP Robinson

Twiceborn

Secrets of Versailles
Book 1

"I had a hard time putting it down." -Emma F., Reviewer

Twiceborn
(Secrets of Versailles I)

SOME SECRETS CAN KILL

Versailles is the center of European power but the court of King Louis XIV is also a hotbed of intrigue and political manipulation.

Despite the rigid structure of Angélique's upbringing, temptation proves stronger than her principles. She gives birth to twins, Antoine and Hugo, who are ripped apart by their mother's shadowed past.

Twenty-five years later, Antoine is caught in a web of intrigue when his jealous brother, now a powerful member of the clergy, accuses him of treason and threatens to destroy the woman he loves.

But Hugo has bigger plans than just his brother's downfall. He ignites a plot that threatens to bring the Kingdom of France to its knees, little suspecting the cataclysmic forces his actions will unleash.

Tears will fall, blood will flow and, in the end, only one man will remain standing.

Buy your copy today.

JPRobinsonBooks.com